BABY SIGN LANGUAGE

How to Teach Your 6-Month-Old Baby Sign Language Today!

Olivia Michael: BABY SIGN LANGUAGE BOOK: How to Teach Your 6-Month-Old Baby Sign Language Today!.

Print Edition 2024©

TABLE OF CONTENTS

Introduction 5

Chapter 1 Embracing Baby Sign Language 9

Chapter 2 Unlocking Cognitive Benefits for Your Baby Explore the cognitive & emotional advantages of early sign language ....

Chapter 3 Early Learning and its Lifelong Impact. Understand Why Starting Young is Crucial for Development & Success ....Error! Bookmark not defined.

Chapter 4 A Journey Through History: The Origins of Baby Sign Language . 18

Chapter 5 Debunking Myths: Answers to Common Questions 23

Chapter 6 Kickstart Communication: Your Baby's First Signs Five Simple Steps to Baby Sign Mastery ....Error! Bookmark not defined.

Chapter 7 Essential Signs to Start with you Baby……………..………....25

Chapter 8 Expanding Vocabulary with more Amazing Signs 39

Chapter 9 BONUS Baby Signs for Potty Training 54

Chapter 10 Let's explore more signs 69

Fun Animal Signs 71

Conclusion 83

A message From the Author Olivia Michael with personal Insights & Encouragement 83

Disclaimer 86

Works Cited 88

Copyright © 2024 by Olivia Michael

All rights reserved. No part of this publication may be reproduced, distributed, or transmitted in any form or by any means, including photocopying, recording, or other electronic or mechanical methods, without the prior written permission of the author, except in the case of brief quotations embodied in critical reviews and certain other noncommercial uses permitted by copyright law.

This book is published by Olivia Michael, and it is protected under the international copyright laws. It is illegal and punishable by law to copy, distribute, or create derivative works from this book in part or in whole, or to contribute to piracy of this work.

© 2024 Baby Sign Language How to Teach Your 6-Month-Old Baby Sign Language Today! Amazon Print edition REVISED 2024.

Introduction

Emma was taught her first 5 signs at six months, and it made both her and our lives much easier.

Instead of crying or screaming, she could tell us when she was hungry, thirsty, needed her diaper changed, or she was just tired.

She learned another 15 signs by nine months, and that was amazing. Now she is talking so much earlier than other children in her preschool, and it's all because of her baby sign language.

Baby sign language gives you a sneak insight into the mind of your amazing baby. It also allows your baby to show you some of the things they are thinking and feeling and lets you share some of your thoughts with them.

During the days of early childhood, where every giggle and gaze holds profound meaning, a remarkable development is taking root among perceptive parents.

This trend is the adoption of baby sign language, a gentle yet groundbreaking approach to nurturing your child's early development.

As we embark on this enlightening journey through the realms of neuroscience and child psychology, let us delve into why introducing baby sign language around six months can be a transformative experience for your baby's brain development.

The Science of Early Brain Development

To appreciate the impact of baby sign language, it's essential to understand the incredible plasticity of an infant's brain. In the first few years of life, a child's brain forms new connections at a breathtaking rate. These connections, or synapses, are the building blocks of cognitive and emotional development. The more diverse and enriching the experiences during this period, the more robust these connections become.

Baby Sign Language: A Catalyst for Brain Growth

Baby sign language emerges as a powerful tool in this context. When you teach your baby to sign, you're not just giving them a way to communicate basic needs. You're engaging them in a multi-sensory experience that stimulates their brain regions involved in language, memory, and motor skills.

This early exposure to a form of structured communication can enhance cognitive abilities, boost vocabulary acquisition, and even foster emotional regulation.

The Benefits: Beyond Just Communication

Enhanced Bonding and Reduced Frustration: By giving your baby the means to express themselves before they can speak, you're opening a channel for deeper emotional connection. This early form of communication can reduce frustration for both baby and parent, leading to a calmer, more contented home.

Boost in Confidence and Social Skills: Babies who can communicate through signs often show increased confidence and curiosity. They become keen observers, eager to interact with their environment and the people in it.

Foundation for Early Literacy: Research suggests that babies exposed to sign language show a heightened interest in books and storytelling, paving the way for early literacy skills.

Promoting Inclusivity and Empathy: Introducing sign language can be the first step in raising a child who is attuned to different modes of communication, fostering empathy and inclusivity from an early age.

Starting the Journey: Tips for Parents

Begin with Basic Signs: In this book, we will start with simple, everyday signs like "Diaper" (Nappy for my UK friends), 'eat', 'drink', 'more', and 'all done'. Use them consistently in the appropriate context to help your baby make these connections.

Be Patient and Observant: Every baby is unique. Pay close attention to your child's responses and progress, and adapt your approach accordingly.

Make It Fun and Engaging:

Use toys, books, and songs to make the learning process enjoyable. Remember, the goal is to enrich your baby's experience, not to overwhelm them.

Connect with a Community: Join groups or forums where you can share experiences and learn from other parents who are on the same journey.

A Gift of Early Empowerment:

Incorporating baby sign language is more than a trend; it's a profound gift you can give to your child. It's about laying a foundation for effective communication, cognitive flexibility, and emotional well-being.

As a parent, you have the power to unlock the boundless potential within your baby's developing brain. Embrace this opportunity with enthusiasm and watch as your little one blossoms into a confident, communicative, and compassionate individual.

In this remarkable chapter of your child's life story, you're not just a caretaker but a catalyst, sparking a lifelong love for learning and connection.

So now, let the journey begin!

Chapter 1

Embracing Baby Sign Language

We have all taught our babies some of the basic sign language, without even thinking about it.

Very simple signs like waving 'bye-bye', clapping their hands to express their happiness and delight, shaking their head for 'no' or pointing to look at something…

Well in short that is the most natural form of communication and that is all baby sign language.

While our babies have this huge desire to communicate their needs, and their thoughts and express their feelings, they lack the ability to clearly do this with us.

This is because their development of speech lags way behind the amazing cognitive ability that our primitive mother instinct has provided us all.

Our babies' hand-eye coordination develops far sooner than their speech, so gesturing is such a basic and natural way for our babies to communicate with us.

Baby sign language builds on their natural instinctive form of communication and allows our babies and toddlers to effectively communicate with us.

Research now shows that babies who use sign language often get a great start in life, exhibiting an increased vocabulary and more advanced cognitive skills, even long after they've stopped signing. Your baby can learn simple signs for basic activities like sleep, eat, milk, more, play, and teddy bear, well before they can produce understandable speech.

Imagine knowing exactly what your baby wants before they can talk, reducing their frustration, and encouraging their cognitive development.

Picture this scenario:

It's 2:30 AM, and your 6-month-old is crying in her crib. When you ask what's wrong, she signs by placing her arms across her chest—a sign for her teddy bear. You hand her the bear, "Baloo," and she falls back to sleep with a smile.

It's surprising how much we use signs in our everyday lives, often without realizing it, as a result of our expressive nature. This instinct goes back to our Paleolithic ancestors and is still a part of us today.

According to Albert Mehrabian, a researcher in non-verbal communication:

Face-to-face communication is composed of:

55% Nonverbal cues,

38% Tone of voice,

and only 7% actual words

"Diaper" is one of the first signs you can teach. It signals when it's time for a diaper change. Soon, your baby will learn to sign "diaper" to communicate this need, reducing frustration and crying. As they advance, you can use the sign to ask them, "Do we need to change your diaper?" This fosters their ability to communicate effectively and respond to questions.

Chapter 2:

Unlocking Cognitive Benefits for Your Baby

One of our most fundamental desires as humans is to be understood.

Extensive research has shown that baby sign language can massively reduce frustration for your baby, and you, by providing a means of communication before they develop speech.

Baby sign language has numerous other benefits for your baby, including advancing their verbal development and strengthening their cognitive skills. Baby sign language helps enhance parent-child bonding by reducing both their frustrations and yours, all through the enjoyable time spent teaching sign language to your baby.

It reduces fussiness; much of this is caused by your baby simply needing something from you but not being able to communicate their need directly. When your baby can tell you when they are hungry, thirsty, need a diaper change, or they are hurt, you can help them.

They feel secure and safe; this early communication is highly bonding and makes you and your baby feel happy, comfortable, and secure. Even when there is nothing you can do, if your baby's leg hurts, this early communication seems to soothe their pain, just by sharing this with you.

Many parents report that their signing babies have a much easier time with frustrations later, like the terrible twos. This alone is a good reason to teach your baby sign language. Latest research confirms that babies who sign have fewer temper tantrums. Parents and caregivers feel much better too – parents of signing children report feeling more positive about their babies, who also seem more content.

Preventing prolonged crying becomes easier as you bond with your baby, but it can still be challenging to decipher exactly what they want. Is it a diaper change, a soother (or dummy, as known in the UK), thirst, hunger, tiredness, or discomfort from being too hot or cold?

Imagine if your baby could sign to communicate their needs, such as "I'm too cold," "I want my teddy," "I'm hurt," "I'm tired," or "I'm wet." This not only reduces guesswork but also enhances your baby's problem-solving skills. Being able to communicate with you during activities or outings is incredibly valuable.

Research in the field of baby sign language has shown that babies who sign tend to develop a stronger bond with their parents. Some early childhood education programs have recognized this benefit and have begun to include baby sign language in their curriculum, helping to foster a solid foundation in the parent-child relationship from the start.

Reflecting on personal experiences, I remember the anticipation of wanting to understand my daughter Megan's thoughts and feelings. The wait until she could verbally communicate at around two years old seemed so long. This desire to connect and understand is a common feeling among parents, highlighting the significance of early communication tools like baby sign language.

When Megan was four months old, I discovered baby sign language and realized it could be a wonderful activity for us to do together, enabling us to start communicating early. By the time she was five and a half months old, I began teaching her basic signs.

To my delight, she picked them up quickly. This period was an incredible bonding experience for us, bringing us even closer than I could have imagined.

Now at three years old, Megan is remarkably advanced. She has an impressive vocabulary and shows strong problem-solving skills, achievements I attribute to the early introduction of baby signs.

This early learning experience has been invaluable – it's more than just a developmental tool; it's a powerful way of enhancing a child's growth.

I cherish every moment we spent together during those early learning stages and am grateful for the impact it's had on her development. Baby sign language is a simple yet profound tool that I wouldn't hesitate to use all over again.

Chapter 3:

Early Learning and its Lifelong Impact

Understanding Why Starting Young is Crucial for Development and Success

To achieve more than 100 billion neurons (the typical number for a newborn baby), the brain must grow at a rate of about 250,000 nerve cells per minute throughout pregnancy.

More on this below.

In the Womb

Early Development: The brain begins to form just three weeks after conception. By the end of the fifth week, the basic structure of the brain is already in place. Rapid Growth: During the fetal stage, neurons (nerve cells) develop at an astonishing rate.

Complexity and Connectivity: By the time of birth, a baby's brain contains almost all the neurons it will ever have, approximately 100 billion. These neurons start creating connections with one another, forming the networks that underpin all bodily functions and cognitive processes after Birth.

Explosive Growth: The first few years of life are crucial for brain development. Although a newborn has nearly all the neurons they will ever need, these neurons are not yet fully connected.

Synaptic Development: The connections between neurons, known as synapses, develop rapidly after birth. At its peak, the cerebral cortex of a two-year-old child will have over 100 trillion synapses. Use It or Lose It.

As the child grows, 'synaptic pruning' occurs, where unused neural connections are eliminated, and frequently used connections are strengthened. This process makes the brain's functioning more efficient and is influenced by the child's environment and experiences.

The Wonder and Opportunity for Parents

The incredible pace of brain development from the prenatal stage through early childhood presents a unique and powerful opportunity for all parents.

Shaping the Brain: Every interaction, whether it's talking, singing, playing, or even cuddling, is crucial in forming and strengthening the synaptic connections in a child's brain.

The quality of a child's experiences and interactions plays a significant role in their brain development. This underscores the importance for all parents to provide enriching interactions.

Critical Windows of Opportunity: Certain periods in a child's development are 'critical windows,' times when the brain is especially receptive to learning specific skills, such as language, emotional control, and motor skills. Parents have a unique opportunity during these windows to enhance their child's development through engaging and relevant activities, such as baby sign language.

Long-Term Impact: The experiences and environment a child is exposed to in their early years can have a profound and lasting effect on the structure and function of their brain, influencing their learning, behavior, and overall health well into adulthood.

The Role of Nutrition and Health: Proper nutrition, regular health checkups, and a safe, nurturing environment are vital for healthy brain development. Parents play an essential role in ensuring these basic needs are consistently met, supporting their child's physical and cognitive growth.

In Summary: The rapid development of a child's brain from the prenatal stage through early childhood is extraordinarily remarkable.

This period goes beyond physical growth, playing a pivotal role in laying the foundation for a child's cognitive, emotional, and social capabilities. For parents, understanding and actively participating in this incredible developmental process is crucial.

It highlights the importance of providing a loving, stimulating, and secure environment for their children, setting the stage for a lifetime of learning, well-being, and overall development.

Chapter 4

The Origins of Baby Sign Language

1800s: William Dwight Whitney discovers children in deaf families outperforming hearing peers.

1980s: Dr. Joseph Garcia rediscovers BSL and starts teaching signing to hearing families.

1990s: Prof. Acredolo & Goodwyn's research shows that BSL works and that there are enormous benefits.

2000s: BSL is gaining widespread acceptance as the evidence mounts.

In the 19th Century, William Dwight Whitney a 19th-century American Linguist had very curious observations discovering that the children of deaf parents can communicate earlier than the children of hearing parents.

Whitney, a Yale professor and editor of comprehensive early dictionaries, recognized and began to remark on the superior communication abilities of children with profoundly deaf parents.

These children, despite having parents who did not speak, learned to communicate through sign language. Whitney's initial observations and findings, however, were not extensively explored and remained largely uninvestigated for over a century until their rediscovery in the 1970s.

In the 1970s, Dr. Joseph Garcia, who was an ASL interpreter at the time, made significant advancements in the field. He observed that the children of his deaf friends were able to communicate with their parents using sign language as early as five and six months old. Remarkably, these children developed a substantial vocabulary by the time they were nine months old.

This was astounding as most babies didn't start even saying their first one or two words until 12 months old. Dr. Garcia actually wrote about this phenomenon in his 1986 graduate thesis.

Shortly after Dr. Garcia began researching the use of sign language to teach children of hearing parents, Professor Linda Acredolo observed her daughter exhibiting simple signs.

During a pediatrician visit with her 12-month-old daughter Kate, they were in the waiting room when Kate approached a fish tank and started blowing air towards it. Puzzled by this behavior, Linda took Kate home for a nap after the appointment.

As she settled Kate in her crib, Linda activated a mobile with beautiful fish that appeared to "swim" when she blew on it. Linda realized Kate had made a connection and was communicating using her own form of sign language, without any formal instruction.

Linda began to wonder: How many other gestures or signs was Kate using to communicate? Were there any other signs that she was making that Linda just hadn't noticed?

Do other children also communicate through gestures or signs? This question sparked Linda Acredolo's extensive research journey. Over the next 20 years, she and her colleague Susan Goodwyn, both Ph.D. holders at the same university, embarked on the first comprehensive studies in baby sign language.

Their research, funded by a grant from the National Institutes of Child Health and Human Development, enabled them to track developmental progress at various ages. These studies and experiments revealed significant benefits of baby sign language for a child's development.

They compared the progress of babies who used sign language with those who didn't, monitoring them at ages 2, 3, and 8 years. The findings of Acredolo and Goodwyn were remarkable. They conclusively demonstrated that teaching babies to sign leads to more advanced brain development and a host of positive benefits.

In numerous comparisons, babies who used sign language consistently outperformed their non-signing peers in various developmental areas. The concept and practice of engaging babies with baby sign language have evolved significantly since the 1800s, beginning with William Dwight Whitney's early observations.

Pioneering researchers like Joseph Garcia, followed by Susan Goodwin and her research partner Linda Acredolo, began exploring the use of manual gestures with pre-verbal babies in the mid-1800s. They focused on the fact that before about 18-24 months, a typically developing child hasn't yet acquired the motor skills necessary for verbal speech.

Essentially, their physical development hasn't progressed to the point where they can articulate words using their mouth and tongue muscles.

However, by as early as 6 or 7 months, most babies are already developing control over their larger muscles, known as gross motor skills. Signing, unlike verbal speech, primarily utilizes these gross motor skills – the control over their hands that a 6-7 months old baby is beginning to acquire.

One significant benefit of teaching basic baby sign language is the dramatic reduction in frustration and crying it can bring. Teaching baby sign language often involves using American Sign Language (ASL), which is recognized worldwide and used by parents and caregivers. ASL signs are known for being iconic, meaning they visually resemble the object or concept they represent, making them simple and intuitive to learn.

A great example is the ASL sign for "MILK," which involves simply opening and closing your fist as if milking a cow. Now, you know the sign for "MILK" and can likely perform it correctly. This demonstrates how straightforward it is to learn baby sign language using ASL.

One of the biggest advantages of using standardized ASL signing is its application in playgroups. When your baby uses ASL, they can start communicating with other parents, caregivers, and babies, fostering early social interactions.

This concept is quite straightforward, isn't it? Another important aspect to remember is that ASL is the third-most-used language in the United States, following British Sign Language (BSL) and Spanish.

Moreover, most high schools and colleges now recognize ASL as a fully-accredited foreign language, meeting the foreign language requirements for graduation. Therefore, using ASL signs with your baby not only aids in their current communication but also provides them with a foundation for learning a foreign language from as early as 6 months old.

Looking ahead, it's clear that baby sign language will be increasingly recognized as crucial for our children's development. It plays an important role in promoting language acquisition, early learning, and literacy, benefiting children universally.

Chapter 5

Debunking Myths: Answers to Common Questions

Certainly, there are some common questions and myths regarding baby sign language. Let's address a few of them:

Does baby sign language delay a baby's ability to learn spoken language?

No, this is not true. Consider this simple analogy: as our children grow, they hit important milestones, such as rolling over and then crawling. We don't worry that crawling will prevent them from walking; it's all part of progressive development. Similarly, signing is a bridge to developing good speech, expression, and overall excellent communication skills.

Can baby signs increase a baby's IQ level?

Yes. Research has shown that signing can enhance a child's speech and cognitive abilities. An eight-year-old who learned baby sign language as an infant, on average, had an IQ 12 points higher than non-signers. This is a significant indicator of the impact of early sign language acquisition.

Can baby sign language help children with developmental delays or disorders?

Yes, there is evidence that signing can greatly aid children with developmental delays and disorders such as Down syndrome, speech apraxia, and autism spectrum disorder (ASD). While there are over 600 signs that can be used for non-verbal communication, starting with just **50 signs can significantly aid your baby's development.** This book can serve as a useful training aid, offering a resource to return to as your child grows and develops.

Chapter 6

Kickstart Communication: Your Baby's First Signs

Here's a step-by-step guide to introducing your baby to sign language, streamlined for clarity:

Getting Started:

Begin with a few basic signs. My top ten selection of baby signs is a great place to start. As your baby starts to sign back, shower them with praise and encouragement. Gradually, as they master the initial signs, you can expand their sign language vocabulary. Start with simple signs and, as they improve, introduce more complex words or phrases. You'll notice that as they learn to say the word, the signs will naturally decrease in use as they transition to spoken language.

Five Simple Steps to Baby Sign Mastery:

Start Small: Choose 2 to 5 signs from my top 10 selection. First, say the word, then demonstrate the sign clearly and naturally. Repeat often.

Contextual Learning: Show the sign in relation to activities like eating, diaper changes, or while handling objects like milk or a teddy bear.

Encouragement is Key: Always praise and encourage your baby, even if their initial attempts at making the sign aren't perfect.

Incorporate Signs into Daily Activities: Use baby sign language during reading or singing to pique your baby's interest.

Follow Your Baby's Interests: Notice what catches their attention and use signs related to those interests for quicker and more effective learning.

Keep it Simple: Start with the basics. Once your baby learns a couple of signs, you'll find they catch on quickly. Progress at a steady pace, introducing about two to three new signs per week.

Utilize Resources: Repeatedly refer to this book as a guide for proper teaching techniques.

Enjoy the Process: This is a wonderful opportunity to bond and develop your relationship with your baby. The results of this shared experience can be truly rewarding.

Remember:

Do not correct your baby's initial attempts at signing. If you can interpret their attempt as the intended sign, that's good enough. They are forming brain connections and developing skills. With time, their motor skills and sign techniques will refine. Teaching your baby at 6 months old also expands their memory. Continual praise will encourage their enthusiasm for signing, improving their skills over time through practice and repetition.

Chapter 7

Essential Signs to Start with you Baby

Core signs every parent should start with for daily communication

Baby Sign for "Diaper": To make the sign for "Diaper," position your hands around your waist. Bring the index and middle fingers of each hand together, then tap them on your thumbs. Some people might do the sign slightly higher up on the body to ensure the baby sees it clearly.

Remember: Keep It Super Simple (KISS): Start with basic signs. Once your baby learns a few, they tend to pick up new ones more quickly, allowing for steady progression.

Baby sign for "Milk" This sign is a lot like milking a cow, but **without** making the vertical motion, you are just squeezing the udder. You take one hand, make it into a fist, relax, and repeat. You may notice your baby may have trouble moving all fingers, but any kind of repeated squeezing and relaxing of the hand is likely that they want milk. Remember: - First you must say the word, then Repeat – Repeat -

Repeat, both clearly and naturally EVERY TIME when you make the sign and when doing the activity.

Baby sign for "Eat" "Food" This sign is a simple, by taking your strong hand and forming a flat, ASL letter O, then tap your hand to your mouth once. To make the sign for food you do the above but you tap your hand to your mouth twice. Verbs are signed once while nouns are signed twice.

Baby sign for "Mommy / Mom". This sign is open palm and five fingers moving back and forward from your chin. Please remember to say the word as you're doing this too. Remember: - First you must say the word, then- Repeat- Repeat both clearly and naturally, EVERY TIME when you make the sign, and when doing the activity.

Baby sign for "Daddy / Dad". This sign is like mommy but higher on your forehead, with open palm, and five fingers moving back and forward from your head. Remember all of the female sign's mom, and grandma are below the nose, the male signs dad and granddad are above the nose... Remember: - Show the sign in relation to what activity or task you are doing.

Baby sign for "Grandmother / Grandma" This sign is like mommy but open palm and five fingers moving back and forward from your chin and do a little 2-step movement downwards. Please remember to say the word as you're doing this too. Remember: - Use the baby sign language when you read or even when you sing with your baby, this will stimulate your baby's interest in the book or the song you are singing.

Baby sign for "Grandpa / Granddad" This sign is like a grandma but higher on your forehead, with an open palm and five fingers moving back and forward from your head with the same little 2 step movement downwards. With continual praise, their techniques will improve over time through practice and repetition, and their enthusiasm for signing will grow especially for the complex signs.

Baby sign for "Sleep" This sign is full hand and open fingers over your face then draw down your face to a closed hand ending just below your chin and also closing your eyes. Remember to say "sleep" as you do the sign. Remember: - First you must say the word, then Repeat – Repeat - Repeat, both clearly and naturally EVERY TIME when you make the sign and when doing the activity.

Baby sign for "Dog" This sign is so easy, by patting your outstretched hand with your fingers together on the side of your hip. It's just as if you were calling the dog to you. (Please note in ASL, the patting of the hip is followed by bringing your hand up and clicking it). We don't do this second step with Baby Sign language. I found that clicking was just a bit too complicated for my baby.

Baby sign for "Cat" This sign is made by flattening out your hands and then bringing your thumbs under to make an O shape. Then, bring your hands together and separate them repeatedly. It's like you are stroking your whiskers. Remember: - This is an amazing time for you and your baby, HAVE FUN, and enjoy this time to communicate, bond, and develop your relationship together.

Baby sign for "More" This sign is easy and is done by, flattening out your hands and then bringing your thumbs under to make an O shape. Then, bring your hands together and separate them repeatedly. I liken this to two birds kissing, repeatedly it's the same motion. You can encourage the more correct form of flattening out their hands and creating the "O" shapes with their thumbs this is a fun way to help them develop their fine motor skills. Remember: - Show the sign in relation to what you are doing.

Baby sign for "Happy" This sign is made by taking your extended hand and brushing it in little circles up your chest a couple of times. The sign for "happiness" is similar to the sign for being excited.

Remember: - Have Fun, relax, and enjoy this amazing time.

Chapter 8

Expanding Vocabulary with more Amazing Signs

Broaden your baby's sign language skills with additional essential signs

As an addition, I've included more advanced signs for your baby. As your child develops these advanced signs are great to further develop your baby's expressive side and will allow them to share with you their thoughts and their feelings.

Baby sign for "ball" Put your fingertips from each hand together with your palms facing inwards. You should look like you are holding a small ball in your hands. Move your hands together and apart, so your fingertips touch then separate.

Baby sign for "book" When your baby signs this for the first time it's magical. This sign is made as it looks hands together center and opens like a book, so easy and a great way for you to know your child wants to hear a story and select their favorite book, 'even before they can read or speak'. Remember: - Use the baby sign language when you read or even when you sing with your baby, this will stimulate your baby's interest in the book or the song you are singing.

Baby sign for "Hat" To sign Hat this is both easy to teach and your child. Tap on your head using your strong hand, as if you are putting your hat on. That's it, simple.

Baby sign for "Teddy Bear" (also can mean) **"Hug" & "Bear"** This sign is made by making your hands into claws and crossing your arm with one hand on each shoulder. Now scratch up and down with each hand. Babies are often going to simplify this into just giving themselves a bear hug. The hug sign is made by making each hand into a fist and crossing your arms over one another. This sign looks like you are giving yourself a big hug. Remember: - First you must say the word, then Repeat – Repeat - Repeat, both clearly and naturally EVERY TIME when you make the sign and when doing the activity.

Baby sign for "Baby" This sign is made by crossing your arms with your hands facing up, one arm is resting on the other while you touch your elbows. Like you are cradling a baby in your arms. Gently moving your arms from side to side.

Baby sign for "Bath" This sign is made by making a fist with both hands while sticking your thumbs out. Move your fists vertically up and down your chest. Its looks like you are scrubbing yourself with both hands as if you are taking a bath.

Baby sign for "Light" This sign is made by taking your strong hand and raise it to your head. Take your fingers from touching each other to fully extended outwards. So this looks like a light is flicking on shining its rays.

Baby sign for "I Love You" This sign is made by putting up your thumb, index finger, and little pinkie finger. Do this while, keeping your third and fourth fingers (your ring finger and your middle finger) down. Hold your hand out, with your palm facing away from you, and move it back and forward slightly. What could be better than exchanging this sign 'I love you' with your baby. Remember to Keep it super simple, (KISS). Start with the basics, when your baby learns a couple of signs they start to get it really quickly, and then you can progress.

Baby sign for "Brother" This sign is made by making both hands into an "L-shape" with your thumb and index finger extended. Hold your weak hand down by your chest. Take your strong hand and starting at the forehead, bring the hand down to your weak hand. When your baby is getting started, brother gets simplified a lot sometimes the "L-shaped" hands will look more like fists, and your baby will often only do the motion with one hand. The sign can sometimes get confused for daddy.

The real bonus here is getting an older sibling involved in teaching baby sign language, this is a great way to get both children engaged. Older brothers love to teach the sign for brother. Have them make the sign whenever they are around the baby. Siblings are often highly motivated to get the baby to sign their name first and will put in a lot of work with the baby to make it happen, so don't be surprised when the baby's first sign is brother or sister. Remember: - First you must say the word, then Repeat – Repeat - Repeat, both clearly and naturally EVERY TIME when you make the sign and when doing the activity.

Baby sign for "Sister" This sign is made by extending your thumb and index fingers on both hands. Take your strong hand and start with your thumb under your jaw. Then move the strong hand and tap it down on top of your weak hand. Remember: - First you must say the word, then Repeat – Repeat - Repeat, both clearly and naturally EVERY TIME when you make the sign and when doing the activity. I repeat that reminder on these two signs above especially because of their complexity and similarity.

Baby sign for "Don't like" This sign is made by taking your strong hand and touching your middle and ring fingers to your thumb while extending your pinkie and index fingers. Starting with your hand at the opposite chest, move your hand away from your body extending all your fingers. The look of utter disdain is optional, but is really fun! This

50

is a great sign to teach your baby to help get them some control over their life and surroundings. To teach the don't like sign, use the opportunities where your baby has an unpleasant experience. Trying new foods is a good opportunity. You can use this when your baby tastes a new food and spits it out, making the don't like sign. Also consider this: Letting your baby acknowledge and express when they do not like something often makes your baby more open to new experiences.

Baby sign for "Please" This sign is made by taking your hand with your fingers extended and all together with your thumb extended and sticking out. Take your hand with your palm facing inward and rub it in a circle on your chest. Remember to say Please as you're doing it. Remember: - Keep it super simple KISS, start with the basics when your baby learns a couple of signs they start to get it really quickly, and then you can progress.

Baby sign for "Thank You" This sign is made by, extending your fingers and thumb. Touch your fingers to your chin and bring your fingers forward. It is almost like you are blowing a kiss out, without blowing and the sign is a bit slower. Remember: - This is an amazing time for you and your baby, HAVE FUN, and enjoy this time to communicate, bond, and develop your relationship together.

Chapter 9

BONUS Baby Signs for Potty Training

Specific signs to support early potty training and foster independence

In the exhilarating journey of parenting, one of the most transformative milestones is potty training. Traditionally embarked upon in the toddler years, a pioneering approach is gaining momentum - initiating potty training through baby sign language as early as six months. This chapter delves into the scientific underpinnings and practical benefits of this trend, offering a compelling guide for new parents eager to foster their baby's accelerated development.

The Science Behind Baby Sign Language and Early Potty Training

The brain of an infant is a marvel of potential, developing at an astonishing pace. In this period of rapid growth, introducing baby sign language for potty training taps into the brain's natural plasticity. This method harnesses the baby's budding ability to understand and use language, enabling them to communicate their needs before they can articulate words.

Studies have shown that children who learn sign language often develop enhanced language and cognitive skills. These benefits extend to potty training, where the early communication develops not only physical readiness but also psychological preparedness for this significant step.

Benefits of Early Potty Training Through Sign Language

Reduced Frustration and Stronger Bonding: Babies who can express their needs through signs experience less frustration. This early form of communication deepens the bond between parents and children, creating a more harmonious environment.

Promoting Independence and Confidence: Mastering potty training signs gives babies a sense of autonomy and achievement. This early taste of independence can boost their self-esteem and eagerness to engage in new learning experiences.

Cognitive and Emotional Development: Learning sign language stimulates areas of the brain responsible for language and cognition. This stimulation can accelerate mental development, contributing to overall intellectual growth.

Health Benefits: Early potty training can lead to fewer diaper-related issues and promote healthy bathroom habits.

Implementing Baby Sign Language for Potty Training

Start with Simple Signs: Introduce basic signs like 'Diaper' "Wet" "All done". Demonstrate these signs consistently and in the relevant contexts to help your baby associate the signs with the action.

Be Patient and Consistent: Every child's developmental timeline is unique. Consistency and patience are key in helping your baby learn and use the signs effectively, and they will.

Encourage and Celebrate Successes: Positive reinforcement plays a crucial role. Celebrate your baby's successful communication and attempts at using the potty, no matter how small.

Integrate Signs into Daily Routines: Incorporate the signs into your daily routine to make them a natural part of your baby's life. This could include signing during diaper changes.

Conclusion: A Pathway to Enhanced Growth and Early Independence

Teaching your baby sign language for early potty training is more than a practical tool; it's a profound opportunity to boost their development and independence. This approach not only eases the potty-training process but also sets the stage for enhanced communication and cognitive skills. As a parent, you're not just guiding your child through an early milestone; you're laying the foundation for lifelong learning and self-confidence. Embrace this journey with excitement, and watch as your little one strides confidently into new stages of growth and independence.

I've talked about baby sign language as a major advantage to teach your baby incredible communication skills. Using baby sign language and using the method of communication for potty training is a major benefit.

I want to share with you the 8 main signs you can teach your baby to develop their communication and awareness for potty training.

All these and more are available in my Baby Potty Training Book. I want you to understand that baby potty training is a gentle, natural, noncoercive process by which a baby, preferably beginning in early infancy, (around 6-12 months old), learns through the care and loving assistance of their parents and caregivers to communicate about and address their E.C. elimination communication needs.

This practice then makes conventional potty training almost unnecessary, making an easy 1–3-day transition from diaper to potty/toilet trained at about the age of 12 - 18 months old.

Parents and caregivers who practice E.C. using baby sign language are often surprised by just how quickly they begin to experience clear and consistent communication with their infant.

Many traditional cultures around the world have known and used these methods for centuries.

Many Western culture parents start to look for supposed signs of "readiness" for potty/toilet training when baby sign language and E.C. babies who have used this method have already achieved toilet independence. "Let's go use the potty" Your baby reaches their hand up and shakes it, using their version of the ASL sign for Potty/toilet (which is the thumb between the index and middle finger then shake your fist). "Let's go!" You say, and you head for the toilet, they sit, still smiling and signing "Potty". "Yes, we're going to the potty".

After a few minutes, they move their arms out, showing that they are "Finished - all done". They get down, their diaper is put back on they wash their hands then they get on with their day. They don't always actually get to the potty but they are 11 months old and enthusiastic about the process.

As we continue with it, the successes are more frequent. I don't see any reason why they shouldn't be fully potty trained by 15 months old. The strategy here is to teach babies how to communicate effectively and start and finish potty training before they are 2 years old.

Fact: There is evidence that potty training a baby under the age of 24 months is actually easier than potty training an older child.

Why I hear you say?

Because as our children get older, they want to make more and more decisions on their own, yes, we have all seen these signs of little Miss or little Mr. Independence.

This natural progression towards independence is healthy, but it can also often set the stage for a battle of wills especially when it comes to potty training.

Alway use ASL baby sign language, ASL (American Sign Language) as this develops consistency, especially if they are cared for by grandparents, daycare, or at nursery.

There is some conflicting information that states there is no need to teach your baby sign language, as they develop their own instinctive ways to let you know what they want through their own method of signing.

My theory is that if we can build on their cognitive ability to use their motor skills first and have a consistently recognized sign language, then there is no doubt of what your baby is saying and it can be recognized by all.

Parent, Grandparent, Daycare worker, etc. Using baby sign language with your baby for their development and potty/toilet training is better for your child. Amazing for Your Child's Development. Potty/Toilet Training not only gives your baby freedom from diapers, but it also gives your baby the benefits of signing as well.

You have the simple methods here to develop your child's natural ability to want to toilet train earlier. There should be no more diaper rash, more independence for the baby, and more flexibility for nursery, daycare, or preschool.

These alone are smart reasons for potty/toilet training your child. As we have discovered ever since the introduction of disposable diapers in the early 1950's, the average age for potty training keeps climbing higher and higher.

Today, the average age at which Western children complete potty training is higher than at any time in history: 36 months for girls and 38 months for boys. Potty / Toilet training your baby before the age of 2 means that you will prevent between 1500 and 2500 diapers from entering landfills.

Just think about that, you can help the environment and save money!

I have included the 5 main signs to start with your baby to develop the E.C. Elimination Communication for Potty training your baby.

Remember you start to teach this sign when your baby is 6 months old. This early communication is a major help to avoid a lot of crying, frustration, and fussiness.

As your child advances you can use this sign as a question. "Do you want your diaper changed?"

Baby sign for "Diaper" This sign is made by taking your hands and placing them down around your waist. Take your index fingers and middle fingers together from each hand and tap them on your thumbs. Some people may do the sign a bit higher up on the body if necessary for a baby to see it properly. Remember: - Keep it super simple, (KISS) Start with the basics, when your baby learns a couple of signs they start to get it really quickly, then you can progress.

Baby sign for "Potty" The sign for potty is made by putting your thumb through your forefinger and index finger and palm facing outwards then shaking your hand side to side. This sign can also be used for 'Toilet'. This sign can initially be used when you read your baby their potty book when you show your baby how to use the toilet, and then when you first go and buy their potty. You will see how quickly they will use this sign to tell you initially they are going to the toilet, and then they want to go to the toilet or potty.

Baby sign for "Wet" The sign for wet is made by reaching up with your hands and bringing your fingers and thumbs together while pulling down. In the beginning, your baby can use the wet sign to tell us when they have a wet diaper and need their diaper changed. Then as your baby progresses, they will use the potty sign to determine when they need to pee.

Baby sign for "All done" This sign is slightly more complex so we start with the sign for FINISHED. This is made by starting with your hands in front of you, your palms facing inwards to each other. Turn the palms so that your hands are facing out. This is a great sign for potty training but can also be used for various other activities like eating and drinking to prevent them from sitting in front of their plate. "Are you all done?"

If you want to do the actual all-done sign, you can see it in the picture above. You take your strong hand and pull it across a horizontal weak hand. It is like you are pulling the curtain on a show because it is all done.

The sign for "PEE" is made by using the ASL sign for the letter P and tapping the on your nose. You can use **"Diaper"** as a general sign, or use this, as if you are discreetly asking your baby if they need to go to the potty.

Sign the letter 'P' by making your dominant hand into a fist, with your pointer finger up and your middle finger extended at a 90-degree angle. Then tap your middle finger on your nose. This is a little more advanced, but gives you options for which one you want to use.

Baby sign for "Poop" This sign can be used independently or you can use the potty sign as a general sign for needing the toilet. We start with your hands in front of you, your strong hand like a fist with your thumb up then you other hand like a fist and insert your thumb into your other hand. You then pull your thumb out of your other hand.

Baby sign for "Wash hands" The sign for wash hands is made by making both hands into a fist, holding the two fists together, and twisting the two fists back and forth. This sign is a must for your baby and a vital habit they must start early. Use the wash hands sign after they use the potty but before you wash your baby's hands.

Also, babies can be a little fussy when it comes to washing up before meals, so doing the sign beforehand can help make them become better prepared.

Baby sign for "Clean" is signed exactly like the sign for nice. All you do for clean is repeat the action two more times. With your dominant hand in front of you palm down, your other hand wipe across your hand with the flat of your palm.

Chapter 10

Let's explore more signs

Baby sign for "Car" The sign for car is made by making both hands into a fist, holding the two fists in front of your chest and moving clockwise and anti-clockwise about 12 inches apart. Like you are holding a steering wheel of a car. See below for **Truck and Bus.**
TRUCK   **BUS**

Baby sign for "More" is made by taking both your hands bringing your thumbs and fingers together like a bird's beak, bringing your hands together and pulling apart repeatedly.

Fun Animal Signs

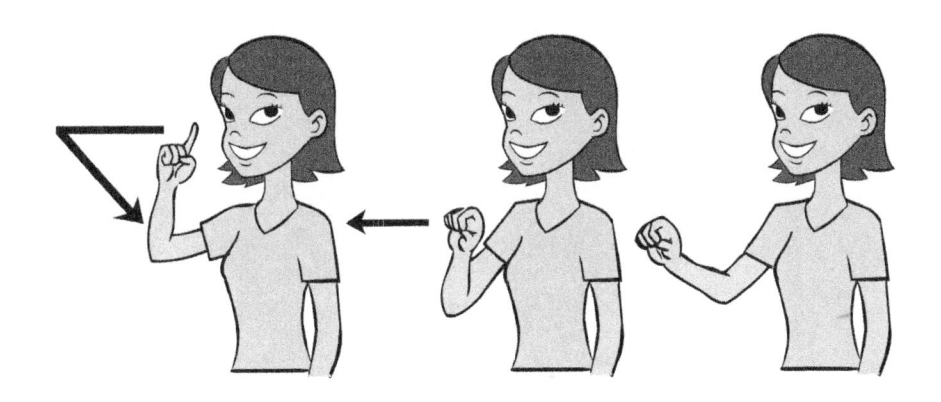

The sign for "Zoo" is like outlining the word ZOO with your index finger. Nothing complicated but this gets your child forming letters and air drawing.

The sign for "Lion" is like you are a lion running your paw through your own mane. Start by making your strong hand into a claw shape curing your fingers and apart. Now take your hand and with your palm against your head run it from your forehead to the back of your head.

The sign for "Giraffe" is like outlining the long neck of a giraffe. Use your strong hand and make a U shape. Now with your palm hand facing towards you, start from your neck and run your hand up ending above your head.

The sign for "Monkey" is basically copying a monkey arm movement in front of your body moving them up and down left and right, sound is optional ☺. This one is fun. Parents love this one especially. Kids always laugh out loud.

The sign for "Hippo" is to extend your pinkie and pointer fingers on both hands and open and close them making it look like a big hippo's mouth.

The sign for "Owl" This involves making your hands into circles and hold them up in front of your eyes. You then twist your hands in and out copying the eye movement of owls.

The sign for "Elephant" Start with your open and slightly curved hand at your nose, then trace the path of your imaginary elephant trunk down and away from your body..

The sign for "Alligator" This is signed by taking both hands open and chomping them together. Like the jaws of an alligator. For added effect extend your arms copying the alligators' long jaws. Make sure to curve your fingers and make them look like sharp teeth.

The sign for "WHALE" is using your non dominant hand and position it horizontally in front of you. Like the surface of the water. Now with your dominant hand hold the middle three fingers out (making the ASL for W) and move your hand over and under the water.

The sign for "Shark" is using your dominant hand all fingers pointing upwards and make a fin on the top of your head.

The sign for "Favorite" using your strong hand bring your hand up to your chin, palm facing you and with your middle finger towards you. Move your whole hand in and out tapping your chin.

The sign for "Fish" This sign looks a lot like a fish swimming through the water. Take your strong hand, extend your hand with your fingers straight and together and your thumb up. Moving it forward and side to side like a fish swimming.

Conclusion

A Message from the Author Olivia Michael with Personal Insights and Encouragement

Well, this is an excellent start for your baby, as the sign above says, Thank You.

I want to extend this thank you to YOU for reading my book. I tried to keep it short, as I know we as parents have a premium on our time, and need all the help we can get!

I sincerely hope you have found it valuable and are enjoying the amazing new experiences with your baby.

That's the basics and by now you should be well on your way to making your baby contented and more comfortable with their new communication skills and abilities. You will by now have the ability to communicate for the first time successfully and allow your baby to perform simple conversations with you.

The signs used are from the ASL American Sign Language.

I really do hope you enjoy this amazing opportunity to share this with your baby and help them grow, watch out for the new book due for release from the Author Olivia Michael with loads more advanced signs, further up-to-date research, and information to make this an amazing experience for you and baby easy.

I am constantly striving to improve your experience when you read my publications.

Please email me your valued comments, suggestions, and feedback at oliviamichael.author@hotmail.com and/or review my book with your comments through the retailer you purchased. I promise I will reply to every email. Thank you for your incredible support.

Please email me your valued comments, suggestions or feedback to: oliviamichael.author@hotmail.com

Thank You Olivia Michael

Baby sign for "Bye" This sign is the same as the traditional gesture for the word. Open your palm, folding down your fingers, and then open your palm again. This sign is a great sign to teach your baby initially and you can use it with baby and friends.

You will obviously know this already, so you can see how natural this is. As guests or family members leave the house, they sign goodbye to your baby, and your baby learns to make the sign back.

BABY SIGN LANGUAGE BOOK: How to teach your 6-month-old baby sign language Today!. Kindle Edition 2024©

Images of baby sign language provided by kind permission of https://babysignlanguage.com/

Disclaimer

The information in " Baby Sign Language, How to Teach Your 6-month-old Baby Sign Language Today! Amazon Print edition revised 2024" is provided as is and while it is written to provide accurate and up-to-date information on the subject matter covered, the author and publisher make no representations or warranties with respect to the accuracy, applicability, fitness, or completeness of the contents of this book. The information contained within is strictly for educational and entertainment purposes.

The facts and data presented in this book are a compilation of various sources, and while every effort has been made to ensure their accuracy, the author and publisher cannot guarantee that the content reflects the most current research and findings. Readers should also note that historical and scientific interpretations and conclusions may vary and are subject to change.

Any reference to people, entities, events, or locales is intended purely to illustrate the subjects discussed and should not be taken as factual representations. The author and publisher shall not be liable for any loss, injury, or damage allegedly arising from any information or suggestion in this book.

The views and opinions expressed are those of the author and do not necessarily reflect the official policy or position of any associated agency or government body.

This book is not intended for use as a source of legal, business, accounting, or financial advice. Readers are advised to consult with a licensed professional for advice concerning specific matters. © 2024 Baby Sign Language How to Teach Your 6-month-old baby Sign language Today! Amazon print edition REVISED 2024.

Works Cited

The research conducted by Dr. Linda P. Acredolo (Professor, U.C. Davis) and Dr. Susan W. Goodwyn (Professor, California State University) revealed long-term benefits of symbolic gesturing during infancy, showing that children who used sign language as infants had a 12 IQ point advantage at the age of 8.

The research conducted by Dr. Linda P. Acredolo (Professor, U.C. Davis) and Dr. Susan W. Goodwyn (Professor, California State University) has been influential in the field of infant development, particularly regarding the use of symbolic gesturing or baby sign language. Their work has provided valuable insights into the relationship between gesture and speech in children's communication.

Goodwyn, S. W., Acredolo, L. P., & Brown, C. A. (2000). Impact of symbolic gesturing on early language development. *Journal of Nonverbal Behavior, 24*(2), 81–103. https://doi.org/10.1023/A:1006653828895. p,13 pp,18-20 p, 22

A related study, "The nature and functions of gesture in children's communication" by M. Jana and Susan Goldin, while not directly authored by Acredolo and Goodwyn, reflects the broader scope of research in this area, highlighting the significance of gestures in children's communication 05e12d682382344c2b84cd45bb2e711989499893†source.

Positive Impact on Language and Cognitive Abilities: Fuller, Newcombe, and Ounsted conducted a study, "Late language development in a child unable to recognize or produce speech sounds," where a child introduced to a manual sign system at 6 years 9 months showed improved communication, reading, writing, conversational skills, and social responsiveness despite initial challenges with speech sound recognition and production. This study suggests that manual sign systems can have a positive impact on language development and cognitive abilities. (Fuller et al., 1983).

NICU Interventions and Long-Term Outcomes: Brignoni-Pérez et al.'s study, "Listening to Mom in the NICU: effects of increased maternal speech exposure on language outcomes and white matter development in infants born very preterm," investigates the effects of maternal speech exposure in the NICU on preterm infants. While not directly related to baby sign language, it highlights the importance of early language exposure for brain development and language outcomes (Brignoni-Pérez et al., 2021).

Baby Gym and Infant Development: A study by Febriyanti, Nurlintan, and Hudhariani, "The Benefits of Baby Gym on Development of Baby Age 6 Months," found that baby gym positively influences the development of 6-month-old babies, as indicated by increased developmental scores. This study focuses on physical activities rather than sign language but underscores the importance of early developmental interventions (Febriyanti et al., 2020).

Language Development in Children: A study by Muluk, Bayoğlu, and Anlar, titled "A study of language development and affecting factors in children aged 5 to 27 months," explores language development in early childhood. This can provide indirect insights into the potential impacts of early communication methods like sign language (Muluk et al., 2016). Reference to symbolic gesturing or baby sign language.

Printed in Great Britain
by Amazon